Dream Interpretation for the Mystical Soul

Pamela Cummins

ISBN-13: 978-0-9976703-7-0

Contents

Dedication

May you use the wisdom of your nighttime messages to accelerate your personal and spiritual growth!

Introduction

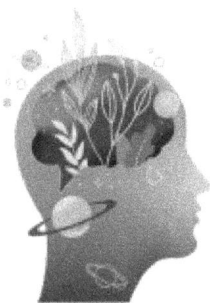

Did you know that dream interpretation can change your life for the better? I know this for a fact, because it happened to me, my clients, and my students. When you understand your dream meanings, it helps you to figure out who you are, and what steps to take in your life.

I've always been fortunate to remember my dreams almost every day and thought some of them were hilarious. 1989 was the year I began my personal/spiritual growth journey, and working on my issues caused me to remember two or more dreams daily. Some of these dreams pointed to my childhood issues. My Higher Source sent me an excellent therapist, who was a dream analyst, and assisted me through some major issues. Unfortunately, my former therapist was very uncomfortable and freaked out when my dreams became more spiritual and predicted the future, so we went our separate ways.

The nature of my spiritual dreams may have upset my former therapist, but they were a spectacular gift for me. After a while, my spiritual dreams seeped into my daytime living; and returned my psychic abilities I had repressed as a child.

My life changed for the better when I practiced dream interpretation. As my dreams' messages alert me to issues to work on, give guidance for my life direction, and connect me to higher beings and deceased loved ones. Dreams also provide solutions for my business, relationships, and health.

Have you ever discovered something that inspires you? You just have to share it with the world, right? This is how I feel about dream interpretation.

I adore the different dream categories; for example, solution dreams, recurring dreams, and even nightmares, as they all have the value of guiding us humans to grow. However, my heart belongs to the spiritual dreams categories.

What type of person practices dream interpretation for their mystical soul? Someone who has a knowing and/or connection with a Higher Source, whom they may call God, Goddess, Jesus, Buddha, or the universe. This person has an open mind and thinks outside the box. Perhaps they know everything happens for a reason. They may have experienced synchronicity, intuition, psychic visions, mediumship, dreams of the future, or dream visits from a deceased loved one.

As a mystical soul who is a dream interpreter, I attract these types of women, men, and LGB&T from all ethnicities. Whether they're Christian, Jewish, Hindu, Muslim,

DREAM INTERPRETATION FOR THE MYSTICAL SOUL

Spiritualist, Wiccan, or have no religion. These people come to me because they need to know their dreams are valid, understand their spiritual dreams, and know what to do with their dreams' wisdom.

I wrote this book to assist you in going deeper into dream interpretation to expand your personal and spiritual growth. You will learn techniques to interpret dreams. Plus, how to use the following to enhance dream interpretation:

- Yoga
- Meditation
- Intuition
- Card readings

This book also features:

- Death dreams
- Deceased loved ones' visitation
- Dreams of the future
- Different characters in dreams
- Past life dreams

Since relationships teach us about ourselves and help us grow, I included a chapter on love relationships.

FYI I've written a ton of articles and blogs, many of these were about dream interpretation. In this book, I've shared pieces from those blogs and articles. Although they won't be the same as the original because they went through a bunch of updates.

The best way to absorb all this information is to read the book from front to back. However, if you feel guided to go to a particular chapter first, trust your guidance. To receive more value from this, it's important to practice and integrate what you learned from this book into your life.

Now, it's time to go explore our nighttime dreams...

Chapter One
Dreams for Spiritual Growth

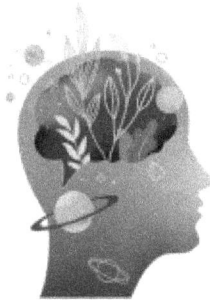

Our planet Earth is a magnificent schoolroom where there is a variety of education. One of the toughest lessons to learn in this classroom is to break free of society's conditioning on how to live our lives. *To thine own self be true* is simple to say, yet it's difficult to live. For many, this unlearning process only occurs during their sleep thanks to our dream state's disregard for conscious rules; instead, it prefers spiritual rules.

Breaking free of society's conditioning is an important step toward your spiritual growth. Although spirituality has different meanings for everyone, a broad definition of spirituality is discovering the purpose of your life, taking the steps to do the work that makes your heart sing (as long as it doesn't harm others), and assisting others on the planet.

Besides spiritual growth, it's imperative to work on your personal growth. What is personal growth? It is facing and clearing up childhood issues, stopping addictions and/or inappropriate behavior, dealing with life obstacles, and expressing emotions appropriately instead of disregarding them or acting out. Obviously, this isn't an overnight process, nor is it smooth sailing.

Fortunately, dreams are here to help you. Dreams provide guidance, solutions, and therapy for a lifetime. If you continue to ignore your dreams' messages and issues, then your dreams will knock louder with nightmares, recurring themes, and/or post-traumatic stress disorder dreams. Therefore, it's worth the effort and time to learn the secret language of dreams.

Dream Interpretation to Accelerate Your Personal Growth

Many people desire to know what their dreams mean. While a few others think dreams are total nonsense. Did you ever wonder why we dream? The following sentences are from the blurb for my book *Learn the Secret Language of Dreams* that delivers a clear meaning of why we dream:

Do you know that your dreams are special and unique? But if you don't understand their meaning, you are missing out on vital information. Because every night your subconscious mind sends you messages to help you solve problems, improve relationships, and teach you how to create a higher quality of life.

DREAM INTERPRETATION FOR THE MYSTICAL SOUL

We are here on the planet Earth to learn, grow, love, and transform into our fullest potential. Although we often become bogged down in the material world. Ta-dah! That's where our dreams of the nighttime come in handy, to remind us why we truly are alive. Life isn't about owning another home or car; instead, we are here to work on our personal growth to become higher spiritual beings. Your dreams reveal four vital facts:

1. Issues/obstacles that need to be overcome.
2. Solutions to every area in your life.
3. The true reality of your life; for a dream will bypass your denial.
4. What your genuine emotions are regarding a situation in your life; stuffing your feelings is not an option in the dreamtime.

If you don't know what to work on, it's impossible to grow; therefore, you need to learn to interpret the wisdom of your dreams. **This is not an overnight process.** Learning your personal dream symbols and messages can be compared to personal growth, which is a lifelong journey... You can't find the full meaning of a dream nor who you are in a book, neither on a blog, or taking a course, although these are helpful tools to assist you to go through the journey of interpreting dreams for your personal growth.

An overview of the work needed to interpret your dreams is:

- Remember your dreams.
- Record your dreams daily or as much as possible.

- Learn your unique symbolism; hint, you *won't* find it in a dream dictionary.
- Discover the patterns and repetition of dream themes. Hence why a dream journal is a must to refer back to.
- Compare your dream to what has happened in the past or is occurring in your life today to uncover possible dream meanings.
- Interpret your dream, while being open for several interpretations.

Yes, dream interpretation requires a mega amount of effort, yet it is so worth it!

Spiritual Dreams Categories

All dream categories are important and serve their purpose. My clients, students, and readers are the most curious and fascinated about the spiritual aspect of dreaming. The three most popular types of spiritual dreams are:

Precognitive Dreams

This dream category is informing you of possible upcoming events, and how you can grow from it is:

- Begin to prepare for the future.
- Make changes to avoid an undesirable prediction.
- Let go and let God (or whoever your Higher Source is) for these events you cannot control.

How does this increase your spirituality?

By trusting the information you are receiving and doing whatever is best for your highest good. While knowing that a power greater than yourself is taking care of you and others.

Dreams of the Departed

Dreaming of your deceased loved ones can assist you in the following ways:

- Knowing that your loved ones are still around you.
- Resolving issues with your departed loved ones.
- Validating that life continues after death.

How does this assist your spirituality?

These dreams will encourage you to work on your personal/ spiritual growth while serving others. You know you will meet again in the afterlife.

Past Life Dreams

This type of dream shows you:

- Why you are the way you are.
- What issues you need to be overcome in your present life.
- Insight into the reason for your and others' behaviors.

How does this speed up your spirituality?

When you ponder your previous lives, you can see what lessons you need to learn in this lifetime. Which gives you the advantage of pinpointing where to grow spiritually.

Another Type of Spiritual Dream

For the last section of this chapter, I'm using a client's two dream scenes for the category of spiritual chapter dreams. This type of dream is similar to graduating from school and becoming ready for the next phase of life. **Please note that the client's dream may not be grammatically correct, as I preferred to have the dream in her own words.**

Spiritual Chapter Dreams

First Dream Scene

I was in a large room, like a large auditorium. There were a lot of people in there. I was sitting on the front row in a metal fold-up chair, when drums started playing. We were taking part in a guided meditation. While the drums were playing, I started swaying in rhythm with the beat. Then I fell to the floor, eyes half-open (kind of like a trance state). I could half see out but I had no control of my body. I was just jerking and swaying, kind of like a fish on the floor. I was half up under the woman's chair that was leading the meditation, and she said to me "get in the egg shape." I balled up in the egg shape (fetal position) except for one leg and I heard someone say, "Kathy, let it go" (Kathy is our 9-year-old daughter). When I finally got completely in the fetal position, she touched me and said, "Now you can be reborn."

Second Dream Scene

After she said that, I was standing on a ledge of a cliff in a horseshoe shaped canyon looking up at several waterfalls. Then all of a sudden the water falls stopped and started flowing backwards. When they did, I started shouting at the top of my lungs. I was so full of Spirit and energy I wanted to explode. I just kept on shouting over and over. I saw a guy I was friends with years ago that I used to attend church with, and we fist bumped.

Then I saw men that looked like Native Americans wrestling and rolling off of the cliffs, but they were not getting hurt. I then turned and saw a large door in the side of the canyon, and I went in. Inside, there were children preparing a lot of food for a large meal. They were arguing and fighting among themselves, and I told each one to love each other and to have peace, and I spoke some proverbs that I really wish I could remember. They just stood there awestruck and agreed with me and went back to work. By this time, I felt like I was glowing.

I walked back outside, and on the edge of the cliff was a gazebo. Inside were 6 or 7 people dressed in traditional oriental attire that was red and black, with what looked like Asian writing all over them. Standing in the center of them was someone that was wearing a solid gold one with black Asian writing all over them. I stood there staring at them and I remember feeling I wanted to stand in the center of them really bad. Then I woke up.

Interpretation for Client's Spiritual Chapter Dreams

The first paragraph is about listening to your own beat and going with the flow. The egg shape is symbolic of birth and beginnings (later validated by the teacher's words). Your daughter is symbolic of **your** inner child and/or inner female (creative, emotional, and intuitive side).

In a nutshell, this dream scene is about letting go of old ways, especially spirituality, since it was in a spiritual atmosphere. And being reborn in spirituality, yet also a new YOU!

Your second paragraph dream scene is going through the process of being reborn! The waterfalls literally cleaned you from the outside and inside. Your shouting was not only about an emotional release, but an energetic release to allow a new way of living and spirituality into your life.

Fist bumping with your old friend is symbolic that it's okay to test out different traditions and spirituality. This was being reaffirmed with your wrestling (Native American symbolism) with testing out different viewpoints on spirituality and ways of life and not getting hurt. Perhaps falling off the cliffs represents going to hell?

The children in your dream represent your inner child preparing to be fed the *new fruits (food) of life*. While their fighting and arguing are symbolic of your inner child; however, intuitively I feel it's for other childish people in your life. Loving yourself and others is the key to peace and feeling the glow within.

The gazebo on the cliff's edge is symbolic of you being safe and protected when you go out on the outer edge of spirituality.

DREAM INTERPRETATION FOR THE MYSTICAL SOUL

At the end of the dream, the people dressed in Oriental attire means to test different types of spirituality to help you get grounded and eventually become centered on higher levels of spirituality.

Now that you, the reader, have a better understanding of how dreams assist your personal and spiritual growth and the different categories. It's time to consider certain aspects when interpreting your dreams.

Chapter Two
Regarding Dream Analysis

There are many schools of thought about how to analyze your dreams. Freudians, Christians, lucid dreamers, Jungian therapists, and metaphysical practitioners all have their theories on how to interpret dreams. And within each group, everyone has their own style of dream analysis. Nobody is wrong in their methods because we are all unique.

My suggestion for interpreting your dreams is to ponder on the emotions, symbols, and actions within the dream. What does a symbol or symbols mean to you personally? How do your emotions affect the symbol and actions of the dream? For instance, dreaming of a snake slithering up your leg could horrify you, although someone who has a pet snake would find it comforting.

Once you comprehend your symbols, emotions, and actions, then it's time to apply them to your life. Is this dream about a current obstacle? Are you being shown the next step to take on your journey? Does it remind you of something from the past, or is it similar to what's happening in your life today? Is this a heads up for the future?

As you can see, dream analysis is much more complicated than understanding what your symbol means. In fact, it could take several lifetimes to fully grasp all angles of dream interpretation. Understanding your dream messages is a journey...

Every one of your dreams has meaning even if it's an environment dream that is alerting you to answer the call of nature. A ridiculous dream has a message for you to figure out. The next section covers this topic.

Do Nonsense Dreams Have Meanings?

A student asked me, "How do you know if it's a nonsense dream or a real dream?" At first, I was taken aback by the question, yet quickly realized that I have a lot more experience in interpreting dreams than she did. Would you like to know my answer?

Here was my answer, "All dreams have meanings, so there is no such thing as nonsense dreams. You just have to learn how to understand their messages." Granted, this is not an overnight process.

If you have a dream that you're dressed in a cheerleader's outfit doing Kung Fu while taking a shower. It has meaning!

Are you wondering how could that dream have any possible meaning? Here's one interpretation:

Stop being a cheerleader to everyone, wash away your people pleasing behavior, and learn how to protect yourself against inappropriate people. As I said, all dreams have meanings.

The idea of nonsense dreams having meaning may frustrate you. And perhaps you're wondering why dreams aren't shown in an easier manner. This quote from my book, *Learn the Secret Language of Dreams,* sums it up nicely:

There is no denial in the dreamtime, only subconscious and spiritual truths.

In other words, human beings have a blanket of denial to protect us from a painful reality. Or we keep ourselves too busy to avoid looking within. Our dreams of the nighttime use codes to help us process our daytime reality and are from a Higher Source that uses spiritual language. Your job is to figure out that language.

Characters in Your Dreams

Characters within your dreams might be who they truly are. But then again, they might not be. Remember, symbols are not straightforward and the same goes for people or any living being. A dog could be symbolic of that perverted man at your local bar. Dreaming of your ex would be easier than acknowledging there are similar patterns in your current relationship.

Reflecting on your characters within the dream is another facet of dream analysis. Then there's the Jungian school of thought that all people in your dream are actually you.

Is Everyone Really You in Your Dream?

In one of my classes, a woman was confused by Carl Jung's concept of how every person in a dream was a version of her or something within herself. Here is my response:

This concept is confusing to most people; we are all one, yet who can see Hitler or Charles Manson within themselves? And what about dreams that are visitation from our departed loved ones?

There are times it's easier to comprehend this theory than others. For instance, I was doing inner child work when my niece was two or three years old (three decades ago); therefore, it was a no-brainer, her character was a symbol of my own inner child. Perhaps you're dreaming about a former teacher you admire, which can be symbolic of your inner teacher, or you are the students' favorite teacher at the school where you teach.

But could you really have the traits of Hitler or Charles Manson? Thankfully, the majority of the population would never commit murder. Nonetheless, dreaming about either one of these men may be symbolic of their characteristics inside of you. Examples of Hitler's or Charles Manson's traits are superiority, manipulation, leadership, organizing skills, or inspiring folks to take action on a cause. Whether these are positive or negative qualities depends upon each person's situation.

Now let's investigate dreams about our loved ones who have taken the journey to the other side. A dream where there's not much talking and/or feels like a visit is usually a visitation from your deceased loved one. When your dream has lots of symbols, scene changes, anger, or other uncomfortable emotions, then more than likely the dream's meaning is versions of yourself or an issue within you to resolve.

Are post-traumatic stress disorder dreams (PTSD dreams) about you? It is difficult to imagine yourself as your perpetrator who harmed you unless there is a part of you that wants to hurt others, or this was a past life dream. Although PTSD dreams are usually about healing the past trauma of an event or events you experienced.

Different dream categories, such as environment dreams or recurring dreams using Carl Jung's philosophy are usually accurate. An example of this is I dreamed my cat told me she needed to urinate, and the princess became upset with my response to go outside because her litter box was at home. Upon awakening, I needed to use the toilet. Recurring dreams are having the same dream repeat itself in an exact or similar fashion, although the people can change. These recurring dreams prompt you to resolve a certain situation in your life.

Precognitive dreams may be premonitions of the future to warn or assist you; hence, it's about you. Yet, this isn't always the case, as many people have dreams of events that have nothing to do with them. Whether it's an earthquake, an act of crime, or a tragic accident occurring close to home or around the globe. A Higher Source has a reason for these folks to dream about these events, even if they may or may not find out the purpose of their dreams.

This theory of you being everyone in your dreams is a fascinating subject to contemplate and is another tool for dream analysis.

Many Meanings of Symbols and Dreams

A symbol in a dream has more than one meaning. Let's take the spider symbol, which may represent creativity, female traits, feeling caught, difficult problems, being controlled by someone, clearing the cobwebs, or weaving a new direction. However, just like the snake symbol, there are hundreds of other possible messages. Even the location will alter the meaning. For example, watching hundreds of spiders crawling up a tree won't have the same impact as hundreds of spiders in your bed!

Since a symbol has many interpretations, so does a dream. At the bare minimum, one dream has at least two different messages, often more. Sometimes all interpretations will feel right to you. While other times your inner ding will go off like the end of a boxing match for the right analysis– ding, ding, we have a winner.

One Dream Has Many Meanings

A few years ago, I was attempting to figure out how to prepare an instruction segment on how to go deeper within a dream and view it from different angles. My mind was having a difficult time figuring out a teaching concept, so I decided to put it on hold until the next day.

It turns out that I didn't have to plan anything as that night I had a dream, which was the perfect example to use for the lesson.

My Dream

My sister, niece, and I were talking in a living room. Cynthia (who's an adult now) was a young teenager and Snowy, their dog who passed, was there. A black leopard was sleeping in the corner, although I felt perfectly safe there. I can't remember much of the conversation except as I was leaving, I commented about the black leopard. My sister responded that she didn't notice it.

I left carrying Snowy, who was on a leash, close to my chest and was walking down a hill. I saw two lion cubs ahead of me and got nervous because I knew the mamma had to be somewhere. Then I heard a lion's roar and thought it was the mother, but when I turned around, it was a male lion. I was too terrified to move as the lion ran toward me and clamped his teeth on my right hand and wrist. I knew the lion could cause serious damage or kill me. So I gave him Snowy to eat, knowing that my niece was going to be furious.

Analysis of One Dream Has Many Meanings

In this section, I will give a simple and deeper analysis as to how it pertains to my family.

Simple Analysis

There's something that I have been avoiding talking about or wanting to do with my sister and niece. I begin walking that path, but I'm fearful of what lies ahead; hence, the two cubs. And how people are going to react. The male lion represents the fact that I need to grab whatever it is by the hand with strength, while sacrificing what my family and others think of me.

Deeper Family Analysis

Cynthia is representing me as a teenager hanging out with my sister. The black leopard is the elephant in the living room aka Denial. My sister is symbolic of my own denial even if bits were peeking out.

Snowy symbolizes the family love and loyalty that I carry within my heart, yet the leash is symbolic of restrictions on my freedom.

The two cubs might be symbolic for my sister and me. My mother wasn't around much because of health issues. Perhaps the male lion is about my father's belief system that was based on his ancestors/society's rules and traditions. If I stand still and allow him to keep a grasp on me, it will limit my creativity and ability to form the life I want to create. So I have to sacrifice something I love or a part of myself in order to move on.

Different Angles of One Dream Has Many Meanings

Now, let's go even deeper into looking within me, rather than focusing on my family.

One Angle

This could be my intuitive and creative female side that wasn't allowed in my family growing up and/or not accepted in society. Even when it's sleeping in the living room! It could also be showing a new journey within my work.

Walking down the hill is me going forward, and it's an easier path. The cubs could be a symbol for two different aspects of my business that will grow... The male lion may be symbolic of not allowing mainstream beliefs to interfere. Or I need strength to grasp the situation and use male logic and strength to build creative projects while feeding them with unconditional love and female power.

Current Life Situation Angle

The black leopard could be symbolic of my black cat, Rhiannon, and/or denial of change within my current household. This enables me to begin to view it.

Walking and holding Snowy could be symbolic of my cat, Merlin, who is also all white. I do walk Merlin on a leash; his name was Snowball before I adopted him; plus I love him with all my heart. The two cubs could be showcasing my two cats or two kittens in the future. Since Merlin has been losing weight and I'm taking him to the vet on Monday. This might mean that I'm going to have the strength to face up to the fact of what a sacrifice it will be for me when he goes to the *Great Big Cat on the other side*—no matter how much it will upset me and my inner child when he dies.

*Merlin passed on February 6, 2021; however, some of the other interpretations were spot on.

How to Go Deeper In Dream Analysis

As I stated before, dream analysis takes time and effort, yet the more you practice, the easier it will become to do. Even a short dream can have many meanings and the need for a deep interpretation.

Going deeper into dream interpretation is so important to truly understand your dream meanings. If you use a dream dictionary app or book, you're receiving a basic viewpoint. Instead, it's important to dig into all angles of the dream. An analogy for you to understand this is when you desire to know your horoscope for the day. There are a mega amount of websites that have horoscopes written from someone's astrological point of view on your star sign. More importantly, these horoscopes are for the general audience and don't take into account the time of your birth, your ascending sign, different houses, and other aspects pertaining to astrology. The same is true for dream analysis.

One Line Dream

A potential client emailed me the following:

So what happens when you dream about driving down the road and you end up sideways?

Now, talk about being general. Any dream interpreter would need more information. For instance, did the car end up sideways? Did your body end up sideways? Did an item in your car end up sideways?

My Response

Your short dream could have many meanings depending upon your emotions in the dream - very important! The type of car you're driving, is it your car from today or a past car, what road you are traveling on, and if you're alone or with passengers? Interpreting a dream is much more complicated than looking up a symbol in a dictionary. I would need more information to do a dream analysis.

Let's look at three different general aspects of how a dream's meaning can change in this dream.

Emotions

- Happiness in this dream could mean not to take things so seriously and to view life from a different perspective.
- While feeling angry may signal to slow down to avoid

becoming ungrounded.

Car You're Driving

- A car from your past might mean that you're holding on to issues that are making your life unbalanced.
- If it's a new car, the meaning can be a warning you to slow down when you are driving.

Who's In the Car?

- Driving alone in the car could be symbolic that you wish for more stability in your life.
- Having a passenger may show you that this particular person is causing havoc, and it's time to take back your power.

The above simple interpretations are just the tip of the iceberg in this dream. Honestly, there can be many more meanings with this short dream using different emotions, the car that's being driven, and who is in the car. Now let's sprinkle in what road they are driving on: a road from their past, the route they take to work each day, a country road, a highway, or a congested road with traffic.

What about your past experiences? Perhaps the dream is pointing to what's happening in your life today? Is there an issue you need to deal with or are you in denial about this issue? Could this dream be a precognitive warning of a future accident?

Now, do you understand why going deeper into dream interpretation is so important? Occasionally it's a simpler analysis. Nonetheless, usually dreams are complicated with many layers and symbolism. This was just a short dream. Imagine a dream that's longer or contains different dream scenes?

After reading this chapter, you now have four different tools to assist you with finding the wisdom in your dreams. The next chapter is about other techniques you can use for dream interpretation.

Chapter Three

Spiritual Techniques for Interpreting Dreams

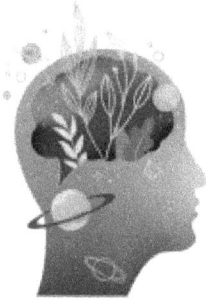

Using relaxing body and mind techniques helps us go into an altered state of mind. Although these techniques might not be as deep as our dream state, they are useful to tap into our intuition and subconscious mind during the waking state. Thus, making it simpler to understand the wisdom of our dreams.

We can compare focused movement in our physical bodies to being in a meditative state. *One form of meditation is to focus on one topic while blocking out everything else.* This is similar to what professional athletes do when they shoot a ball through a hoop or score a goal. An athlete's primary focus is on scoring a goal or getting the ball in the basket, at the same time blocking out the audience's voices and actions.

Intuition also occurs while we are moving our bodies. Did you ever go for a walk and **boom**, a fantastic idea pops into your mind? This flood of inspiration can occur while washing the dishes, taking a shower, practicing yoga, or doing other activities. It's easier to receive intuitive information because your focus is elsewhere. Many folks practice yoga in the morning, which is a perfect time to be open to receiving information about your dream.

Yoga Poses

The following yoga sequence is a method to find insights into your dream's meanings.

- Sit in a lotus or a cross-legged seated position. Breathe deeply as you contemplate your dream.
- Set your intention that you will receive clarity on the dream's meanings at the end of your practice.

Don't focus on analyzing your dream, rather, allow the answers to be revealed to you. To help you with this, *do poses to keep your head below your heart* to prevent you from thinking too much. In each of the following poses, *breathe deeply five to ten times* before moving on to the next one.

Below Heart Poses

- Begin in mountain pose (stand tall with feet touching, arms by sides, and palms of your hands facing forward).
- Do a forward fold (feet together, with knees slightly bent, bend from your hips while moving your hands towards the ground, and place your hands on your thighs, knees, calves, or floor; whichever is more comfortable to you).
- Raise up into a half forward fold (move hands to calves or where it's comfortable, flatten your back, and look forward).
- Move into downward dog (from a standing position or floor, put your arms in front of you with palms on the ground, move your legs back, then go on your toes until your legs and arms are like a triangle, and slowly move your heels towards the ground).
- Put your knees on the floor and move into a seated position. Grab your dream journal, smartphone, or whatever method you choose to use. Record whatever came into your mind, even if it doesn't seem to relate to the dream.

If you're new to yoga, please take a yoga class for beginners or watch videos online to learn how to do these poses properly. Always listen to your body on how far you can go in a pose. Listening to your body and doing the poses correctly will help you avoid injuries.

Answers to Your Dreams

If you receive the answers to your dream's meanings before finishing the poses, you have a choice of two options. The first is to repeat your insights over and over as a mantra until sitting back in a seated position to document the answer. Second, stop the practice to record your dream's meaning, then continue with your practice. Interruptions do happen during a yoga home session all the time, as I can attest to when my cats join me on the mat.

No Insights?

Perhaps you didn't receive an answer? No worries, continue with sun salutations or other poses. Once you have finished with the physicality of your practice, allow yourself to breathe deeply into Savasana (relaxing Corpse pose). Again, don't force an interpretation; instead, let go. You may get an answer during Savasana, later that night, in a couple of days, or while washing the dishes.

Do It Yourself

These poses aren't set in stone, and I encourage you to come up with a practice that is right for you. Or do this with another type of exercise. You could even do this with housework. Whatever helps you to set your intention, focus your mind on something while allowing the dream's meaning to come to you.

Although intuition and meditation are mentioned in the physical aspect, let's dive a little deeper. We'll use intuition to help uncover a symbol's meaning. Then meditation to interpret the dream.

Intuition

If you are unsure of what an image message is, use your intuition for the correct dream symbol's meaning that feels spot on to you. One symbol can have many interpretations. Sadly, many people won't take a moment to reflect on what a dream symbol means to them. They think they will find an instant answer by clicking on a dream dictionary app. I wish it was that easy! If you must do this, please allow your intuition to guide you to choose one of the definitions listed in the app that feels right about the dream. Don't be surprised if none of the definitions applies to your dream symbol. This happened to me decades ago when I researched symbols in a dream dictionary book. The author's interpretations was off on so many of my symbols that I donated her book.

If you are already in touch with your intuition, you may choose to scan or skip the following until you find the two exercises to help find your correct dream symbol's meaning.

Intuition is...

For those of you who are unsure if you're truly in touch with your intuition or if it's just your ego, here are three ways to tell the difference:

1. Intuition is soft and quiet, while the ego is loud.
2. Intuition happens quickly, yet ego keeps going...
3. Intuition often doesn't make sense, but the ego has a million reasons why it's right.

Intuition may occur as a knowing, a gut feeling, or a chill in a warm room. Regardless of how your intuition happens, it's important to learn to trust it. For instance, when you intuitively pick up to:

- Take an umbrella on a sunny day.
- Drive the back roads instead of the highway to go home.

Perhaps there's an accident that causes a traffic jam for hours. Or your car breaks down and it's safer and easier to pull over on the back roads. The reason you take an umbrella was an unexpected rain shower. Or a mugger saw it, realized you wouldn't be an easy target, and picked another victim. You never know!

It takes time to trust your intuition. Don't be surprised when people tell you that your intuition is wrong. It takes practice to disregard their opinion, then follow what's right for you.

Two Exercises for the Correct Dream Symbol's Meaning

Use one or both exercises to find your symbol message.

First Exercise

Close your eyes and take a couple of deep breaths. Then visualize, feel, or just know the symbol is there. Ask what does this symbol means and allow the answer to come without thinking of the answer. You might receive a memory to connect the symbol with, hear a song lyric, see a scene out of a movie, or just perceive the answer.

Continue this exercise for every dream you remember. Until the day arrives when you intuitively know what the symbol message is without doing the exercise.

Second Exercise

This exercise is for those of you who use a dream dictionary app or book. If there is more than one interpretation for a dream symbol, practice each meaning separately. Close your eyes and review the symbol or symbols in your dream. Next, take the dream app's meaning for the symbol.

What does your intuition tell you about this meaning for your symbol? Don't force it, allow the answer to come on its own. You may hear the word no, notice a pressure in your gut, receive a different meaning, or an inner ding of yes this is correct. Continue to practice this with the app/book's other interpretation of your dream symbol.

In time, you may delete the dream dictionary app or toss the book and prefer using your intuition. Either way, please practice exercise one, too.

Remember, a symbol is only one step for dream analysis. Once you become comfortable using your intuition for the correct dream symbol's meaning, take the next step and apply it to interpreting your dreams. Or do the following meditation exercises.

Meditation

When you meditate, your conscious mind is more aware of what's going on than in the dream state. You have a choice of two meditation styles to use. Sometimes you can keep your mind blank and other times you may use visualization. Let's investigate these two styles.

Silent Meditation

- Find a quiet spot where you won't be disturbed.
- Close your eyes and ask for the meaning of your dream.
- Do your best to keep your mind clear without thinking about what the answer could be.
- Allow the answer to come up, whether it is a thought, an emotion, a vision, a smell, or an audible answer.
- Journal the messages you received, even if you don't comprehend them at that moment.

Visualization Meditation

- Find a quiet spot where you won't be disturbed.
- Breathe deeply and close your eyes.
- Visualize your dream taking place.
- Allow yourself to use other senses (hearing, feeling, etc.) if you have trouble visualizing the dream.
- Ask for clarity while you're remembering your dream.
- Let go of how this process happens and allow

whatever comes up in the manner it needs to.
- Journal whatever occurred and/or answers you received.

Delayed Answers

Perhaps you didn't receive any information? Please do not allow this to discourage you, as your fear or anticipation could have blocked the process. Therefore, either wait a few days to repeat this procedure or take a time out. Sometimes, the answer may not happen right away in meditation. Rather, the meditation assists you to receive insight in another manner, such as you receive the dream meanings out of the blue, your dream repeats itself to help you understand it upon awaking, overhearing a conversation, watching a video, or while searching the internet for information on another topic. There are times when you need input from a trusted friend or dream analyst to break through your denial.

A former teacher of mine often stated, "Psyche is kind, it never gives you more than you can handle." If you have not received an answer, it means that it's not time yet. Know that when you're ready, your answer will appear.

There you have it, three spiritual techniques to further your dream interpretation practice. In the next chapter, we will investigate three types of card decks that can assist with dream analysis, and how they are similar, too.

Chapter Four

Card Decks for Dream Interpretation

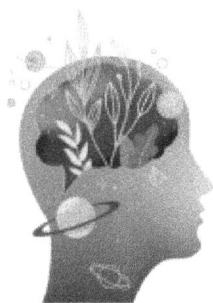

People love their tools, whether that's an actual hammer, a dream dictionary app, or a dream journal. Some individuals use tarot, Lenormand, or oracle cards to help discover the meanings of their dreams. If a student asked me, "Should I buy a dream dictionary or a card deck?" My answer would be to purchase a deck they feel attracted to. Why? Because cards tap into the subconscious mind with their symbolism, pictures, and words.

When you shuffle the cards, then choose the card or cards from the top, or by spreading them out to pick at random, you are allowing the right card to come to you. Please avoid using the guidebook if you don't understand the card's meaning. Instead, examine the card or use the silent or visualization meditation techniques from Chapter Three for the genuine message. Only use the guidebook if you're truly baffled.

You can use a card to clarify a symbol and/or the meaning of a dream. For an even deeper interpretation, selecting additional cards will gain further insights.

A Dream Using Cards

To help you better understand this, let's use Sally's (not her real name) dream example.

Sally dreams about a man she just met at a business meeting. He bends down on one knee and pulls out an engagement ring.

Tarot Cards

Shocked and half asleep, Sally whips out her tarot cards, shuffles, and pulls out the *Lovers* card. If Sally is just learning tarot, she might think, oh my God, I'm getting married! Or that this man is interested in her as a lover. Although if she is a seasoned tarot practitioner, Sally will realize that the Lovers card is about many types of partnerships, and this could be about business.

Sally's feelings in the dream are clues to help clarify the *Lovers* card. When Sally looks at the card, she notices how the man and woman are naked. She thinks back to the dream and ponders how uncomfortable she was when he got down on his knees. The dream's meaning becomes clearer to Sally not to reveal anything about her work project. Perhaps he wants to take credit for her hard work?

Yet if Sally felt good about this man pulling out the ring, the meaning might be to proceed with this partnership in business or romance.

For additional insights to clear up her confusion, Sally draws another card, and it's the *Ace of Pentacles*. Pentacles are about the Earth and material goods. An ace can represent opportunities or new beginnings. These two cards are letting Sally know that their relationship could prosper in business or romance. Still, she needs to use her logic and avoid jumping right into any type of relationship with this man, especially if her feelings were uncomfortable in the dream.

Sally can continue to pull additional cards or use a tarot spread for further clarification on her dream.

Oracle Cards

Those who don't like or can't relate to tarot cards can use oracle decks. Oracle cards usually have words on them; nonetheless, you can receive information from the pictures, too. Before writing this section, I thought it would be fun to choose a card from three different decks for Sally's Dream.

From *The Wisdom of Avalon Oracle Cards* by Colette Baron-Reid, I picked the *Dog* card. This card is all about unconditional love and loyalty. Sally knows they can be in a good partnership. Again, her feelings are clues to this card.

I chose a card from my *Answers from Animals* deck and got the *Ponder the Situation* card with a buffalo lying in the grass. A reminder to take it slow and build the foundation with this relationship.

Mutual Dreams is the card I selected from my deck *Learn Dream Interpretation Cards*. Perhaps the man is having the same dream as Sally and/or the attraction is mutual.

Lenormand

Most of the population is familiar with tarot and oracle cards, but not Lenormand. If you never heard of Lenormand, I'll give you a brief introduction. Lenormand readings began in the late eighteenth century and were named after Marie Anne Lenormand. The Lenormand deck has thirty-six cards, which are read for practical advice and/or divination. Some symbols on the cards are easier to read; for example, heart, key, and anchor. While other symbols are more complicated; such as lily, fox, and bear. Lenormand cards get right to the point. There's no beating around the bush with this deck!

I picked the *Stars* card from my *Merlin's Purrfect Lenormand* deck. One meaning for the *Stars* is fame, and another is Heaven sent. This card is letting Sally know that their relationship will bring popularity. Or the angels have blessed this relationship to help each of them grow.

Did you notice that the cards from tarot, oracle decks, and Lenormand were all positive? When you put them all together, the message for Sally is this relationship is in her life for a reason, to get to know this man, be positive, ponder how the relationship is going, and allow it to grow.

Dream Interpretation and Cards Similarities

Dream interpretation, tarot, Lenormand, and oracle cards all take time to learn. Oracle cards are the easiest to learn. Symbols are clues on all three card decks, yet they can change meanings depending on the additional cards chosen and in different types of spreads. Dreams also use symbols, but there can be many messages based on the actions, feelings, and more in the dream.

Of course, there are differences. Dreams happen while we are sleeping and are nonphysical. A card reading is done when we are awake in their physical forms. We can hold the cards in our hands, but not our dreams. Most people will view them as completely different from one another.

With this in mind, let's look at Lenormand and dream interpretation commonalities.

Three Similarities of Dream Interpretation and Lenormand Cards

Here are three main similarities:

1. Symbols

Symbolism in dreams can be compared to the foundation of a house, as both are needed to build upon, whether that's an interpretation or a home. The symbols in Lenormand are even more important; not only are these symbols the foundation of a house, they are also the floors, the walls, and sometimes the roof.

Symbols in dream interpretation and Lenormand cards are similar in offering an enormous amount of possible messages. Let's use the *House* card as an example.

Samples of the house meanings in Lenormand are:

- Home
- Family
- Heritage
- Home Business
- Hermit
- Roommates

In dream interpretation, a house could be symbolic of:

- All of the above
- Moving
- Childhood issues
- Time to settle down
- A career in real estate
- Your body with different meanings depending on what floor or room you dream of

Nevertheless, there are many more possibilities of what a house could symbolize.

2. Many Meanings

In both systems, there are countless meanings and messages. Symbols are only one part of dream interpretation and Lenormand. Let's look at other factors that are involved:

Lenormand Cards

Besides symbols, there are:

- Card numbers
- Different Layouts
- Cards placement
- Pips (similar to playing card's diamonds, hearts, clubs, and spades)
- Themes – relationships, money, health, and so forth

An example is the *Snake* card.

The *Snake* card has a negative meaning for many Lenormand readers. Some readers view the Queen of Clubs on this card as an excellent businesswoman who is ruthless; for example, the character Miranda Priestly in "The Devil Wears Prada" movie. However, if a three-card layout for the question of *how to grow your business* is the snake, heart, and star – an interpretation could be it's important to work hard at what you love about your business to become well known in your industry.

Dreams

Apart from symbols, it's important to observe the following in your dream:

- Emotions you felt
- Actions in the dream
- Other symbols
- People in the dream
- Past experiences
- Present circumstances
- Potential future
- Dream Categories

Let's use the snake symbol again to demonstrate how meanings change:

In your dream you felt happy holding a snake, it might mean that you're in for a happy transformation in life. Then your ex runs in with an ax and chops the snake in half, causing you to become angry; therefore, the message will change. This could mean not allowing your experiences with your ex to stop you from experiencing a joyful change. Or perhaps it's an actual warning that he enjoys bringing havoc into your life?

3. Enhances Growth

The most important dream interpretation and Lenormand cards' similarities are that they accelerate your personal and spiritual growth. How? By:

1. Solving problems
2. Receiving guidance

3. Inspiring changes
4. Going deeper within
5. Validating your intuition
6. Discovering who you are
7. Trusting a Higher Source

Do you now understand their similarities? Perhaps it will motivate you to learn Lenormand, tarot, or an oracle card deck?

Sleeping with Your Cards

Tarot experts recommend sleeping with cards to help absorb them into the subconscious mind. This can also be done with Lenormand and oracle cards. Sleeping with an entire deck would be uncomfortable. Put them on your nightstand or the floor, and it is okay to leave them in the box or bag. One or several cards can fit under your pillow or in the pillowcase. Or fall asleep with a card in your hand.

Besides your subconscious mind absorbing the cards, it can bring about fascinating dreams!

Now that you know about using card decks to help interpret dreams, let's move on to a topic you don't want to miss. The next chapter is about relationship dreams.

Chapter Five
Love Relationship Dreams

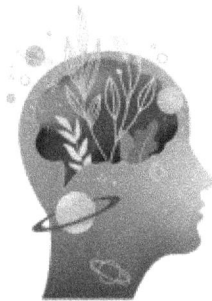

Relationships are where we humans get our greatest education. ~ Pamela Cummins

The above quote is from my first book, *Psychic Wisdom on Love and Relationship,* which was published in December 2012. This quote triggered positive and negative emotions from my audience. One angry man responded by sharing how his divorce wiped out most of his money. Hmm, this was only the surface of his relationship lesson.

As human beings, we have an innate desire to find our other half. A small part of this reason is to keep the population going. Yet an even stronger yearning is the need for companionship, someone who accepts us for who we are, and stands by us.

Some people make wise choices in a partner, while others choose unhealthy relationships.

Dating Dreams

With billions of people on the planet, it would seem logical to think it's easy to find *the one*. Then why can dating be so frustrating? Physical attraction is easy and in abundance, although it's not real. Often we end up feeling empty in this superficial romance. While the spark and deep connection with a soul mate is rare, thus harder to find.

In the beginning of a relationship, we often wear rose-colored glasses or we find ourselves in what I like to call *La La Land*. Our dreams bypass this intoxicating feeling and will give us guidance on whether a person is truly the *Right One*.

* In the following examples, I have changed names to protect the identity of my clients.

Two Red Flag Dreams

First Dream

Janie had just moved to a new area. She had gone out with a man a few times when she had this dream about him:

Women surrounded him and he was touching their breasts, butts, and private areas.

I warned her that this dream was showing her an enormous red flag about this man. It was imperative to take it slowly and get to know him by keeping her pants on. Janie took my advice, and he stopped texting her. Several months later, she discovered his reputation as a player.

Second Dream

Susie had been seeing Harvey for three months, yet they had only gone out six times because they lived far away from each other. Here's the dream she had:

Harvey denied he was drinking a beer, yet he reeked of beer and behaved like he was drunk.

My interpretation was this dream was waving a red flag about Harvey. He most likely has an addiction problem, whether that is with alcohol or something else. Harvey also is in denial about it and has trouble being honest with himself. Her dream was warning her to stay away because Harvey wasn't healthy with his addictive behavior and denial; therefore, he couldn't be truthful with her.

Precognitive Warning Dream

Here's a dream I had many, many moons ago when I was in my late twenties and is in the precognitive chapter of my book *Learn the Secret Language of Dreams*. The people in my dream were all adults in the following dream:

I was in my grammar school gymnasium surrounded by lots of people. There was a nice-looking man with dark hair, a beard, and a mustache. I do not remember the words, but the feeling I got *was that he wanted to control me. I felt like I needed to get away from hi*m.

A few months go by, then I was at a party and the man who was in my dream introduced himself to me. I was shocked, talked to him, and foolishly gave him my phone number. He pursued me very hard and would stop by the places he knew I frequented. I went out on one date and got the same feeling I had in the dream. That date was an important lesson for me because I realized the dream I had was indeed a premonition to warn me to not become involved with this man. I kept my distance and thankfully; he took the hint. I found out later that although he was in his late twenties, he had been married three times! He obviously had issues with relationships and I had no intention of being wife number four.

* Please note that it is uncommon to dream of a stranger who looks exactly the same way they do in real life. Our dreams will use whatever is in our subconscious to carry out the message or warning. What this means is the person in the dream may not be your current potential mate. Instead, you might dream of an ex, a bad boy/girl in a movie, or someone else's undesirable mate. Whoever's face appears in your dream, the information is just as valid whether it's pointing to red flags in a relationship or someone who is not right for you.

Not the Right One or Timing Dream

Billy felt enamored with a woman and asked me to interpret the dream he had about her.

He saw her approaching, but they walked by each other as Billy felt the distance between them.

Now, this dream could have four interpretations:

1. One of them is moving away to a new location.
2. They need to communicate more and work on the relationship.
3. Billy needs to keep on walking by because she's not the right one.
4. Their lives were on different life paths at this time.

Billy felt the fourth interpretation was spot on.

Why Am I Dreaming of My Ex?

I get asked the above question a lot. It makes sense you would dream about them if you broke up with someone recently or a year ago. What frustrates my clients is when they dream of an ex from years or decades ago.

Here are seven dream themes about an ex-spouse or ex-lover:

1. Getting back together.
2. Making love.
3. Catching them cheating on you.
4. Arguing with one another.
5. Feeling the distance between each other.
6. Having a conversation.
7. Healing a relationship issue.

Let's go with the positive dreams first. When you dream about getting back together, making love, or having a conversation, this could be about your desire to be a couple again. A different way to interpret these three dreams are the relationship has not reached a conclusion; in other words, this chapter is not over yet. These also might be precognitive dreams of reuniting as a couple.

The negative dreams of your ex-partner cheating on you, the two of you in an argument, or being distant from one another are spotlighting what is unresolved with one or both of you. These are issues that are hanging on, which need resolution before you can move forward in life or be in a healthier love relationship. Take the time to process your feelings and thoughts.

It is also important to look at what were your flaws in the relationships. Determine why you chose this person and the lessons you needed to learn. Work towards forgiving this person while being grateful for all the gifts you received from your time together. I know this is not a simple process, nor easy to accomplish, although it is worth the effort for the freedom you will receive.

When it comes to healing relationship issues, this type of dream is baffling when the ex is from decades ago and you haven't thought about them for numerous years. These dreams may have symbolism that is difficult to figure out. Or it's easy to figure out, but you're banging your head to comprehend why you're dreaming of this issue. There is always a reason why, although each dreamer's reason depends upon lots of factors.

Often it's an issue you need to heal because a current situation in your life triggered it. This problem could be within your current relationship, a family member, a friend, or a work relationship.

Review what is going on in your present life to determine why your ex-mate appeared in your dream.

The following paragraph from my book *Learn the Secret Language of Dreams* sums it up nicely:

One of my clients was so upset about having dreams about her abusive ex-husband because she was now in a good relationship with a very loving man. She had done much inner work on herself and could not understand why she was still dreaming of him. My guides reassured her the dreams did not mean she wanted him back, nor would he come back into her life. The dreams were to help her cut the final thread of the rope of that type of dysfunctional love to allow healthy love more fully into her life.

Our dreams assist us to process feelings, thoughts, as well as our true heart's desire, which we are either in denial about or too busy during the day to acknowledge. Dreaming about an ex-mate is helping you heal.

Cheating in Love Relationships

These dreams are very upsetting to people. However, are these dreams always about our relationships? Sometimes this type of dream is about another area of your life. For example, being overcharged for a new car and you feel screwed.

Since this chapter is about love relationships, I will focus on cheating dreams as they pertain to romance. Let's go over three types of dream meanings with actions you can take.

Fear of Being Cheated On

If you had a past relationship where your partner was unfaithful to you, this might have triggered your dream. Unresolved issues from prior partnerships could cause suspicion, difficulty trusting, or looking for evidence of infidelity in your present love life. Your dream or dreams are pointing out a need to resolve and heal past events. Here are five tips to assist you:

1. Journal your thoughts and feelings. This will help you to release your feelings of insecurity, rage, tears, or whatever emotion you need to let go of.
2. Start forgiving your ex; remember this is not an overnight process.
3. Look within to discover the truth if you are truly ready to be in this current relationship.
4. Observe your mate's behavior. Are they flirty, working late, staying out all night, or hiding texts or phone calls? Or is your partner attentive, affectionate, or reliable?
5. Consider the need to resolve childhood issues with a counselor or coach.

Dissatisfaction with Your Relationship

When you have been faithful, yet dreaming of having an affair with someone else, the dream is alerting you of being dissatisfied with your love partner. You could be bored, feel neglected, or angry with your mate. This dream is pointing out that changes need to occur in your relationship. Take one or more of these five suggestions:

1. Ask yourself if you still love your other half.
2. Write a list of the pros and cons of your relationship to determine whether you need to leave or stay.
3. Be accountable for what you're doing in the relationship, instead of focusing on their actions.
4. Think about what the two of you used to do during the courtship stage. Then do those things to bring the spark back into the relationship.
5. Focus on what brings your partner joy; however, you should be comfortable with it. Please stop if it makes you feel uncomfortable or degraded.

Warning Dreams

Sadly, there are times your dream of being cheated on has already occurred or it is a precognitive dream that this could happen in the future. Before jumping to conclusions and accusing your significant other, I would suggest using the tip that was suggested earlier in this section by *observing their behavior*. Next use the following five steps:

1. Mention the dream you had and pay attention to their reaction.

2. Listen to the still voice within to determine if your mate has been faithful.
3. Act, don't react. What this means is to release your emotions **before** confronting your partner. You could scream, journal, punch a punching bag, or do whatever to feel centered. This will stop you from doing something rash, which could lead to your imprisonment or being the star of a viral video on the internet!
4. Ask yourself if this relationship is worth saving.
5. Begin the healing process, whether the relationship continues or dissolves.

Should I Stay or Should I Go?

There's no guarantee a relationship will last forever. Some folks would rather stay together because it's comfortable and they fear the unknown. Since relationships should help a couple grow, being in a stagnant relationship keeps them stuck. It is either time to work on the relationship or leave to learn how to become comfortable alone, then attract your next lesson in the relationship realm.

Let's look at two solution dreams.

Time to Move On

Julia was debating whether to continue her relationship with Tom, whom she had been seeing for almost a year. During our session, I recommended asking for guidance right before she fell asleep to receive an answer in a solution dream. Here's her dream:

I was standing at home plate in a baseball field, while Tom was in the outfield. I felt frustrated when I walked towards him, as each time he walked backward further away, this happened three times. After the third time, I walked off the baseball field feeling disgusted.

Even though this dream's meaning is very apparent, I will interpret it. Tom has been playing games with Julia by keeping his distance. On the other hand, she is the one taking the initiative in their courtship. In baseball, you strike out after the third unsuccessful attempt to hit the ball. For Julia, it was much more than three attempts to move forward with Tom; nonetheless, this was a symbol for her to quit any further action. When she walked off the field, her dream was giving her guidance to leave the relationship.

Let's Get This Relationship Started

This is my personal experience and dream. I met my honey on a dating site, where we had been emailing back and forth for about two to three months. In one email, I gave a hint about us meeting in person. His response was for us to continue emailing each other.

His response hurt, which made me wonder if he was already in a committed relationship. So I replied how I needed to think about it and would get back to him. I asked my Higher Source to give me a solution dream of what I should do about this man.

I dreamed I bumped into my honey and said hello. He smiled at me, replied hello, and walked away. I felt his shyness and how much he liked me.

I took this as a sign to continue and then emailed him about how we could continue emailing each other since he didn't want to meet in person. His response was to ask me out. It turned out what I thought was a hint about us meeting missed the mark. Thank God, I listened to my dream because we have been together for over a decade.

Final Thoughts on Love Relationships Dreams

Many of the dream examples used in this chapter were on the negative side. Thankfully, we also have positive relationships dreams once we do the work. This reminds me of wise words from a friend, "Everyone wants to meet *the one.* What they don't realize is often we need the lessons of *not the one* to become ready for *the one.*"

How do we prepare for the one? Use the following tips:

- Stop looking for your soulmate.
- Learn how to love yourself and relish being single.
- Enjoy the time you spend with whomever you're with today.
- Leave someone who is abusive and has unacceptable

behavior.
- Focus on your part when there are problems, not what they are doing wrong.
- Discover better ways to communicate with your partner.
- Accept your partner for who they are.
- Learn the lessons from the relationship.
- Have an attitude of gratitude for your romantic partner.
- Allow the relationship to evolve and go wherever it needs to go.

Loving, successful partnerships are worth it and take effort to continue...

Do you remember my earlier precognitive warning dream about Mr. Wrong? Our next chapter covers dreams of the future.

Chapter Six
Dreams of the Future

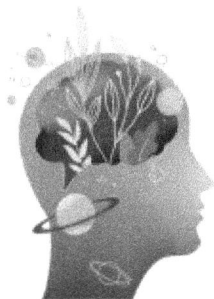

Dreams of the future are also called premonition dreams, precognitive dreams, or what I like to call *a heads-up* dream. Why do we have this type of dream? One theory suggests all time is occurring at once, yet in the physical body, we are trapped in time and space. Therefore, we are really remembering and its déjà vu.

These dreams transpire for different reasons. Let's go over these.

Four Types of Precognitive Dreams

Warning and Protection

Precognitive dreams happen to warn and protect us. My dream about the man in Chapter Five, who had been married three times is a perfect example. If I never had the dream, I might have ignored the feelings I had and became involved in an unhealthy relationship. Having the dream beforehand reinforced my feelings.

Natural Disasters, Tragedies, and Crimes

Another type of warning premonition dreams are about natural disasters, tragedies in the area you live in, crimes, or murder. I used to belong to a psychic group in New Jersey, USA, where many people had a warning dream a few days before 9/11 occurred. Some of these dreams were symbolic, although one person dreamed about planes flying into buildings.

People have warning dreams that don't involve themselves and their loved ones because it is easier for them to handle when hardships happen to acquaintances or strangers. They may need these dreams as a reminder to pay attention to their dreams and psychic abilities. Or for them to use their precognitive dreams to warn others and/or assist the police.

Spiritual Chapter Dreams

Dreams of the future are also used to alert us to our next spiritual chapter in life, which I went over in Chapter One. Do you remember I used a client's spiritual chapter dream where she went into an egg shape, let go to be reborn, stood at the edge of a cliff, then the waterfall flowed backwards, and so on?

This type of dream can be about a new job, career, or business. Perhaps you are moving to another location and/or creating an important change within you or elsewhere. Sometimes you are meeting a romantic partner, friend, or even a pet.

Upcoming Death

When you have a dream about an upcoming death, it can also belong to the warning and protection type of precognitive dreams. However, I feel this should have its own category because of how powerful the death of a loved one's heads-up dreams are and the effects on our lives. Your dream is also a gift to help you spend precious time with your loved one. You might need to make amends to them. Whatever actions you need to take, this will help with closure.

Disregarding or Keeping Quiet

Many often poo-poo their intuition, and it's the same with premonition dreams. Honestly, it can be a little scary to tell others as we don't know how they will take it. They might make fun of us. Or people who dream of a crime can be interrogated by law enforcement when warning the authorities, perhaps even thought of as the perpetrator.

Back in the late 80s, I mentioned my dream to my former boss and co-worker. It was about my female boss talking to her boss that there were issues with the payroll. When lo-and-behold, a couple of hours later my boss lady was ranting to her boss about problems with the payroll! I lowered my head and kept quiet, while I was panicking inside. Thankfully, nobody mentioned the dream.

Since you're reading this, I'm hoping you don't dismiss or will stop disregarding your dreams about the future. My intention for sharing my payroll precognitive dream is to prevent you from revealing your dream to unsafe people. Only tell your dreams to someone you trust and who cares about you.

Who Will Believe Your Precognitive Dreams?

You don't have any control over how a person will react to your dreams of the future. Some people will have faith in them, others will poke fun at your dreams, a person might get mad at you, and ignorant folks may think you're the devil.

My late stepmother, Alison, often had dreams of planes crashing or car accidents. Some of these dreams occurred, while others didn't. Some people took her car crash dreams seriously and took a different route home. One person canceled their flight.

When Alison worked at a pharmaceutical company, one of her co-workers heard about her dreams. He was a MD and had a PHD, too. This intelligent man had enough confidence in her ability to tell her, "If you ever have one of those dreams, please tell me, and I'll cancel my flight."

Four Signs of a Premonition Dreams

Here's how to identify your dream as a heads-up of the future.

1. Your precognitive dreams are more vivid than your other dreams.
2. You've an inner knowing (similar to your daytime intuition) this will happen.
3. You remember the dream even if you rarely have dream recall.
4. Your future event happened in your life which is similar to the dream.

It is not an overnight process for you to determine and understand your four signs of a premonition dream. This is why it's important to keep some type of record of your dreams, which will contain proof of your precognitive dreams. I suggest recording your dream when you have one or more of these four signs. The more you experience precognitive dreams, the easier they become to pinpoint.

Time

Sometimes our premonition dreams occur quickly, other times they don't. A few of my clients' dreams didn't occur until years or decades after they dreamed them. Here are two examples from my clients whose names I have changed.

First Dream

Linda had recurring dreams about her home and moving. A year later, she moved into a new home, and then she realized one of her dreams had shown her what her bedroom looked like.

Second Dream

Julie would have dreams of a man's energy sporadically in her twenties and thirties, but never saw his face. She felt as if this was her soul mate because of the deep connection and love. When Julie met Ted in her early forties, she immediately recognized him.

These two dreams showcase how important it is to allow time for this dream category. Once it occurs in your daytime life, go back to the record of your dream. If you didn't write down the feeling or how you knew it would happen, then visualize the dream to see if it triggers your emotions and/or knowing memories.

Symbolism in Dreams of the Future

Wouldn't it be nice if our dreams played out like watching a movie or reading a book? Our dreams would make more sense if they had a beginning, middle, and ending that was done in our daytime language. As you know, dreams rarely happen this way.

Many times, precognitive dreams have symbolism for you to figure out. Obviously, it is easier to know what the dream meant once the events play out in your waking life. Although I would suggest to look at your dream from different angles that were discussed in Chapter Two. In that chapter, I used a dream to demonstrate the many meanings of one dream. To refresh your memory, the dream was about my sister, my niece, their dog, Snowy, with a leopard sleeping in the corner. Then I was carrying Snowy down a hill where my path intersected with two lion cubs and a male lion.

If needed, use the silent and visualization meditation exercises from Chapter Three. Similar to all our dreams, dreams of the future may also have other meanings too.

Intuition, as discussed in Chapter Three, is very important with these dreams. Before jumping to conclusions, calm yourself down, breathe, close your eyes, and ask yourself the following three questions. Allow the answers to come.

1. Does this feel true?
2. Could it happen?
3. How can I prepare myself in case it occurs?

Pamela's Symbolic Dreams

My two dreams from 2017 are great examples of symbolism, the need to calm down, allow time to occur, and to trust your intuition. I used a tarot card, too.

First Dream

I dreamed I was with Chris and his friend from work at an interesting store. (In our waking life, we have gone out on double dates with his co-worker and wife.) I was having lots of fun, and didn't want to leave.

In the second scene, we are with a bunch of his co-workers in a place that looks like a department store. I felt uncomfortable around these people because I didn't know them. Chris goes off with a bunch of people from work up the elevator, leaving me with two of his male office-mates that I wasn't crazy about. I said, "Where's he going?" One man told me not to worry about it; nevertheless, I felt upset that he left me stuck there.

My dream had a precognitive vibe to it, although I was puzzled over its meaning. I received a text from Chris informing me that we had two opportunities to go out this Saturday, and he wanted to know if I was interested. The first was from our friend who invited us to go to antique stores, but his wife had to work. Our other opportunity was to see a movie, plus go out to eat with a bunch of people from his job. I laughed as I concluded that's what the dream meant, yet it was the wife who was left behind. So I replied yes to the text for going to the antique store and hanging out with his co-workers.

Second Dream

We were at a place similar to a department store; however, it was different. Chris strolled away from me and put his hand on the waist of a pretty young girl. I angrily asked, "What is going on?" His response was, "It's not a big deal because she's my ex-girlfriend." Then he walked away with her and a bunch of other people from his work. When I tried to follow, all of a sudden, an enormous piece of glass appeared and was blocking the way. I was furious!

I awoke feeling very upset and concerned about the dream because of the precognitive energy. I couldn't help but wonder what the message was in these two dreams. Could the second dream be pointing out that Chris liked someone from work or some young girl from work was interested in him?

Tarot and Intuitive Message

After I calmed down and centered myself, I pulled a tarot card on how our relationship was. The card was the "lover's card." Whew! Thank God, yet I still felt fearful.

So, I asked my guides if everything was okay between Chris and me. Instantly, I got a vision of the last scene from the television show "Medium" where her husband gave a choking woman the Heimlich maneuver. I understood that clairvoyant message. You see, in that particular episode, the medium kept having a dream about her husband standing behind a woman that had a sexual vibe to it. Her dream wasn't clear until the end of the show when her husband saved the life of the woman. My vision from this show's scene was to let me know not to worry.

That vision did help me let go of my fear. However, I felt anxious to discover what the dream meant.

Time and True Meaning

I learned the *true meaning* of my dreams when Chris came home with a stomach virus he caught from his co-workers. He spent most of Friday night vomiting, slept a lot on Saturday, and felt better by Tuesday morning.

Interpretation

The first dream was showing my excitement over the upcoming events. But his co-workers' actions would interfere with the events.

In the second dream, my mate touching the young girl represented a new sickness and past illness. When Chris walked away with his co-workers, it was symbolic of being part of those who got sick at work. And the glass blocking the way showed how he distanced himself from me to prevent me from catching the flu.

After Thoughts on Dreams

I did feel disappointed because I would have liked to go antiquing. I was mad at his co-workers for going to work sick and spreading their stomach flu. Luckily, I didn't become sick because we kept our distance.

Can you imagine if I had allowed my fear about this dream to act out and accuse Chris of being with another woman or abandoning me? It would have caused trouble in our relationship! May my dream show you the importance of remaining calm, review a dream from different angles, meditate on it, use your intuition, and allow time – time.

Precognitive Dreams for an Upcoming Death

Part of living is experiencing the death of a loved one, which causes grief and the need to mourn. A premonition dream of someone's death helps you prepare for their death. If you dream that somebody is going to die, does that mean they will? Thankfully it doesn't. Dreaming of someone's death could mean:

- Transformation in your life.
- Lessons that you have learned; in other words, that chapter has ended.
- Prior past life memories.

Signs of Precognitive Death Dream

These are five characteristics (I already mentioned the first three in this chapter) that indicate your dream is a prediction for a loved one to pass:

1. This dream is more vivid than your other dreams.
2. A feeling and/or knowing this event will come to light.
3. You can recall this dream when you rarely remember your dreams.
4. It breaks through your denial of signs that you have been ignoring.
5. As time passes, more evidence appears, whether that is your loved one having health issues or behaving

recklessly.

The Gift of Knowing

Realizing a loved one is going to cross is very upsetting. However, these are the benefits:

- Spending quality time with your loved one.
- Making amends and repairing issues in the relationship.
- Hugging and kissing them.
- Reminiscing about the good times.
- Preparing things for the inevitable.
- Letting them know how much you love them.

Doing the above reduces the regrets of what you should've and could've done.

Pamela's Precognitive Dreams for an Upcoming Death

Loss of a pet can be just as hard as or even harder than losing a human loved one. Our pets are with us constantly in ways that people can't be. Perhaps the shower is the only time I have complete privacy; nonetheless, my cats sometimes wait for me to come out. When Merlin was a kitten, he used to play/attack me while I was in the shower.

My nine dreams assisted me before Merlin's crossing and I will share three of them. Perhaps my dreams will help you in some manner.

First Dream

Merlin jumps up on the bed, purring and rubbing his head against me. The love between us was incredible. I intuitively knew that it was important to spend more time with him, and those were his wishes as well.

Interpretation

Sadly, my heart ached as I knew this was probably a precognitive dream for Merlin's upcoming death. Because a psychic asked me what was going on with Merlin. After this dream, my soul mate, Chris, said he was worried because Merlin was losing weight on his hips and back legs. Chris advised me to make a vet appointment.

Second Dream

This dream occurred before the vet appointment:

On my front lawn, Merlin is lying down in the grass with a gigantic snake around his body and a big leopard sitting next to him. The snake is squeezing him and starts going around his neck. Merlin behaved in a calm and peaceful manner. While I'm freaking out. I'm also terrified as I want to pull the snake off of him, but afraid it will attack and hurt me.

Interpretation

Upon awakening, I knew this was symbolic for Merlin preparing his transformation into the other side and the leopard was his spirit guide. My baby boy felt peaceful about his upcoming transition because he knows that this was a normal part of life. Meanwhile, I'm not okay with his dying. I desired to protect him, plus I'm terrified of going through the pain of his death and life without him.

When I did psychic readings for cat owners aka servants, there was always a theme that cats were purrfectly at ease with the prospect of death. However, their owners were not. Some of these humans put their cats through painful medical procedures, which the cats didn't want.

Third Dream

I'm flipping through a photo album after Merlin has passed (he was still alive at the time), then I come across a picture of me sitting on the bed next to Chris with Merlin laying by my legs in my former bedroom in Morehead City, North Carolina. My hair color is silver, yet I dyed my hair when lived there.

The photo turns into a video that Chris is filming. Rhiannon (my girl cat who is still alive) jumps on the bed and I started singing. I get out of bed still singing and the camera goes for a closeup. My hair is shoulder length, and the color is salt and pepper. Then it closes in on my face and neck area, which has a ton of wrinkles (much more than I have now). I think to myself, boy, did I get wrinkly. But the feeling of happiness is enormous in the video.

Interpretation

This last dream is showing me that life is about the transition from the past, present, and future. To enjoy these moments, spend time, and express myself with those I love, plus to enjoy the lessons/wisdom from life. My life is worth living at any age, while it's filled with happiness and memories.

Believe me, I treasured *every moment* with Merlin before he passed.

May the lessons from my third dream inspire and motivate you to live your life to the fullest. Please spend time with and enjoy your loved one, regardless of whether or not you had a precognitive dream of an upcoming death. When they depart, may you know the tremendous sorrow you feel is worth the tremendous love you had with them.

Now that you learned about my precognitive dreams of Merlin's crossing over to the other side. Can you guess what the next chapter is about? The next chapter is about death dreams.

Chapter Seven

Death and Deceased Visitation Dreams

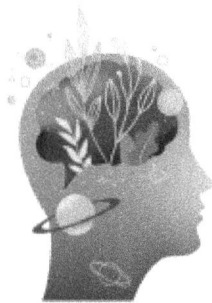

Dreams about dying and death can be very frightening. Some people find dreams about their deceased loved ones confusing and/or scary. My hope is this chapter will help to alleviate your fears and confusion about these types of dreams.

Decades ago, a rumor was going around that if you're dreaming about falling and hitting the ground, you will die. The same would be true if you dreamed that someone murdered you. Supposedly, the shock alone will kill you.

Was this scientifically proven? If it was, wouldn't we also have scientific proof of life after death? Could this rumor have an element of truth? It is possible. But wouldn't the person be dead and how could they pass on this information to the living?

None of my clients ever talked about having a loved one tell them they died this way in their visitation dream. Nor have I spoken to a medium or read in mediumship books about someone who passed because of dreaming about their death.

What I do know is a person can survive being killed in their dreams. How? I experienced two dreams about being shot in the head. Obviously, I didn't die because I'm writing this book.

Meaning of Dying in a Dream

So what does it mean when you die in a dream? It's the same meaning as the Death card in Tarot. The next time you see a movie where the death card appears with scary music playing in the background, please know it's for dramatic effect. What this card represents are endings and transformation.

Endings is a common meaning for your death dream, too. That's right, the ending of a chapter in your life to help you transform and grow to a higher level.

Could a death dream have another meaning? Of course, there's always a possibility of more than one interpretation for your dream depending on your emotions, other symbols in the dream, issues in your life, and past life experiences.

Seven Explanations of a Death Dream

1. A warning of present or upcoming health issues.
2. Your fear of death coming into your dream.
3. Past life memories of your death in a prior life.
4. The recent death of a loved one or acquaintance.
5. An unresolved issue or event that you wish would just *die*.
6. Too much reading and/or watching television about death and murder.
7. An actual precognitive dream of yours or someone else's actual death.

Visitation Dreams

Dreams about your deceased loved ones can trigger a wide range of emotions, from peace to anger, and all feelings in between. A common question I hear is, "I dreamed of my dead mother (father, husband, wife, daughter, son, sister...) last night. Was it an actual visit?" Well, that depends, as there are three types of dreams within the deceased dreams' category. They are:

1. Actual visitation dreams.
2. Unresolved issues with the deceased.
3. A combination of a visitation dream and unresolved issues.

Let's go over the signs of an actual visitation dream and an unresolved issue dream.

Eleven Signs of a Visitation Dream

1. Your dream feels like a visit.
2. There isn't much action.
3. You experience intense feelings of love.
4. No words are spoken in the dream.
5. You and your visitor have a brief conversation.
6. All communication is done telepathically.
7. Your visitor lets you know they are okay.
8. There's a desire to make peace with one another.
9. They use symbolism, yet it is a short dream.
10. There is an inner knowing that this is more than a regular dream.
11. Your loved one is healthier or younger than they were at the time of passing.

Nine Signs of an Unresolved Issues Dream

1. You are dreaming of a past event.
2. There are a lot of dream scenes.
3. This dream **isn't** loving or peaceful.
4. The dream has a lot of action that can be unpleasant.
5. You or your visitor are angry and/or misbehaving.
6. It feels like you are having a normal dream.
7. There is a ton of symbolism in the dream.
8. The dream makes little sense or is totally wacky.
9. Your loved one looks the same as they did during a past event or when they crossed over.

Are the above two lists on how to tell whether it is a visitation or issues dream written in stone? Not necessarily. These are guidelines for you to use.

A Combination of a Visitation Dream and Unresolved Issues

I used to think either your dream is an actual visit or it was used to guide you through an issue. Until I had a visitation dream with a combination of both. After my experience, I started getting clients who had both types within one dream, although there could be more than one dream scene. Why does this happen? These two examples will help you comprehend this.

First Example

Let's suppose you are having a dream about the past when your deceased mother was unsupportive and wanted you to stay with your abusive ex-husband. This dream might have occurred because you still feel hurt and resentment about how your mother believed your ex wasn't abusive instead of believing and helping you.

Your dream now becomes a beacon to your departed mom. Perhaps it's for her own healing, love for you, or heavenly duty to comfort you during your distressing dream. Your mother pops into the next dream scene to help you forgive her, thus bringing peace into your life.

Second Example

This can also happen the other way. Your recently departed dog visits you in the dream to let you know she is okay; for a moment you feel peace and joy that your dog is in peace. Yet, because you feel responsible for and haven't grieved fully over her death, in the next dream scene, you return to the memory of putting your dog down at the vet.

None of these three types of visitation dreams are better than the other. All of them help heal your relationship with your deceased loved one to bring you serenity. However, these dreams aren't a cure for grief. You still need to go through the mourning process.

Visitation Request

Some of my students wish their deceased loved ones would visit them. They wonder why other family members or friends had visitations, and they didn't. Grief can block dreams of the deceased, especially when it's a recent death. Or their departed loved one is still in transition and has heavenly stuff to do.

Whatever the reason, an invitation is in order. An invite is nice for the living, and those on the other side appreciate it, too. Really, it's that simple, just ask them to visit you.

Seven Types of Invites

1. Pray to a Higher Source, God, Goddess, the

Universe, or whatever name you choose to have a visitation from your loved one.

2. Request out loud or silently for them to visit you in your dream.

3. Write your loved one an invitation or type it on your device.

4. Chant it as a mantra; for example, (say their name) please visit me in my dream, (say their name) please visit me in my dream...

5. Visualize sending them an invitation. If you have trouble seeing it, then feel it or just know it was sent.

6. Look at their photo before you go to bed.

7. Sleep with an item of theirs; for instance, clothing, jewelry, or some type of keepsake. You can wear it or put it under your pillow, on the nightstand, or on the floor.

Please be patient and allow time for their visit. Your loved one may visit you in your dreams. Or they may prefer to visit you during the day when you are awake.

Signs of a Daytime Visit

Sometimes your deceased loved one's preference is to visit you in the daytime. The following are two ways they show up.

Through Your Senses

You might sense them. Here are some examples:

- Sense they are around you.
- See or get a quick glimpse of them.
- Feel a light touch or a change in temperature.
- Hear their voice by your ear or inside your head.
- Smell a scent you associate them with, such as cologne, cookies, or cigarettes.

Physical Signs

Other ways your loved one can make contact is through physical items. They could be:

- Pennies or other coins.
- Feathers on the ground.
- Objects moving to another spot.
- Lights flicking or other electronic occurrences.
- Phone calls with their number coming up on the screen.

Whatever way your loved one chose to visit, enjoy the signs from them.

When Do They Visit?

Our loved ones who crossed over to the other side are not trapped in time and space like we are. We Earthlings can have visitation dreams before they pass, right after they died, or months to years after their death. Let's go over the timing.

Before They Die

This type of dream is what I consider a premonition visitation dream. I've experienced this with my mom and two cats, Midnite and Merlin.

The reason we have this warning dream of their upcoming passing is to help us take care of any issues, have closure, and most important of all – **spend precious time with them**. As painful as these dreams are, they are also a gift. The following is a dream I had of my mom back in the early nineties:

I felt someone tugging on my hair and was terrified of who it could be, but turned my head to see who was there. At first, I was relieved when I saw my mom. Then I was flooded with this incredible love that words can't even describe! No words were spoken.

When I woke up, my first thought was my mother was dead. She wasn't. When my sister called to ask if I wanted to go with her to see mom, I knew it was *a must visit*. Our visit was a good one, and I felt at peace with our relationship. My mom died a few days later.

Right after Their Death

This is the most common visitation dream. Some people have their loved ones visit them before they even know they have died. Later, they learn of their passing.

Our deceased loved ones are letting us know they are okay. They also want to ease our grief over their departure. During our mourning, we can reflect on this dream to bring moments of peace.

Months to Years after Their Passing

Sometimes we might not hear from our departed loved one until much later. This can happen for four reasons.

1. Your grief is so intense it blocks them from being able to visit you in a nighttime dreams.
2. You could have had a dream visitation, yet don't remember it.
3. They may need to recover from their death. This is especially true in an unexpected death, murder, or other tragedies. Think of it like a hospital or rehabilitation center. Your deceased loved one may think only hours or a few days went by, while in Earth time it has been months or years.
4. They're busy. A couple of years after my mom passed, I asked a medium why my mother wasn't coming through. I was stunned when the medium replied, "She's busy."

Dream of a Deceased Father

A client granted me permission to use her dream for publication. Just a little background before going into the dream and interpretation; her dad has been deceased for a few decades, while her mother passed a few years ago. This dream also has some symbolism in it.

Dream

My dad appeared to me in our kitchen where I grew up, my son was there, too. At first, I thought my dad was my son because he was so young. He was in his white T-shirt, bathing suit, and black socks. For a minute, it seemed that he was not alive when I hugged him, but then he was.

We went by this watery world where I was before and he was driving on a narrow road surrounded by water. I thought we were going to go in, we didn't, but we were okay. Next, my dad and I were in a store, then he left to do something.

I kept trying to call him on my phone, somehow this guy next to me was controlling it. Then I told that guy to stop it and he did.

I was still trying to call my dad when I saw him walking with his friend. My mom was in the background. He said he lost weight because he didn't have money for lunch.

When he was gone, I was in a salon and the girls kept making comments about their customers. I told them that I knew what they were doing.

Interpretation

Your dream seems to be a combination of a visitation from your father, symbolism, and your feelings about his death. When your dad appeared in the kitchen, he was stopping by to say hello. His appearance was similar to your photo of him in order for you to recognize him. The meeting place was the hearth of your childhood home. Since your son was also there, it is your father's way of letting you know that he is watching over both of you. And he is always alive inside of you; hence the meaning of the hug in your dream.

The water world and narrow road could be part of the visitation, yet also symbolic. Water's main interpretations are emotions and cleaning. For this part of your dream I am interpreting it as you and your dad have made peace with his passing, the road in-between each other is narrow, and he's with you during your ordinary moments, even when you're at the store.

In the next scenes, you are being shown that you can contact your father no matter how it seems out of your control. On the other side, your father is with his friends and your mom is there, too. The weight loss and not having money for lunch stands for him letting go of his Earthly form and needs. What the important message is that *your father and mother are always with you*, as well as other loved ones.

There could be quite a few meanings for the salon scene; therefore, let's keep it in the same context as the other scenes. This is showing you that some people may fear visitations from their departed loved ones, so instead they poke fun at the subject. You are letting them know you understand what they're doing while standing in your truth.

My client's dream is a wonderful example of how our loved ones are with us throughout our lifetime until we meet again.

Dreams about Deceased Pet

It is painful when a pet dies, whether it's a cat, dog, bird, hamster, snake, or another type of animal. Pets are members of our family. They may follow us into the bathroom, love us on a bad hair day, and are a constant in our lives. This is why it's so hurtful when someone tells us it's no big deal they're dead because it was just a cat, just a dog, or just a bird. Death affects everyone differently. Who are we to judge someone's grief over their pet?

A rabbi that I admired lost some of my respect when he was adamant about animals not having souls. This is one of the reasons I wrote the following in *Learn the Secret Language of Dreams*:

There are people who believe that animals do not have a soul, which is a load of garbage! All living things have a soul, have lessons to learn, and evolve. If they breathe, eat, discard waste, feel, love, and have a form of communication (even if we can't understand it), why would they not have a soul like humans?

If your belief is animals don't have souls, then skip this part. For the millions who know their deceased pets are hanging out across the Rainbow Bridge, you may experience a visitation from them. Dreams about our departed pets help ease the loss.

Visitation dreams from our deceased pets also have what was mentioned earlier in this chapter. The different visit timing and the signs of a deceased visitation or issue dream. Sometimes they are just a visit or may have a little symbolism in it. Other times, our guilt or unresolved issues with a pet need to be addressed and resolved.

Signs of a Deceased Pet's Visitation Dream

Each dream of a departed pet is unique to the owner. Here are three examples of visits from pets.

Sleeping with You

Many clients and friends have told me that they feel, smell, or sense their pet on their bed in their usual sleeping spot during their dreams or right before waking up.

Barking

A family member, who is now a cat owner, told me that she dreamed of a dog barking. She woke up thinking that doesn't sound like the neighbor's dog. Then it occurred to her it sounded like the bark from her dog, who had passed away a few years back.

Goodbye

When Merlin, my white cat, was a kitten. I had the following dream:

Midnite was on top of a pedestal and jumped off, then Merlin leaped up to the top of the pedestal.

This was Midnite's way of showing me that she approved of Merlin, happy that I had another kitty in my life, and wouldn't be visiting me as much. The next time Midnite visited was when I sensed her energy. It was a few days before Merlin passed. Perhaps she was there to guide him across the Rainbow Bridge?

Did this chapter ease some of your fears and confusion around death and visitation dreams? These dreams remind us how death is a part of life. Therefore, please enjoy every moment spent with your loved ones and live your life well.

The next chapter covers dreaming about someone else, yet you wonder if it's really you. Is it a past life dream or are you somebody else?

Chapter Eight

Is It You?

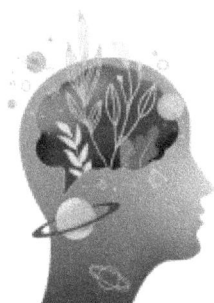

Have you ever had a dream where you looked different, yet you knew it was you? If you're male, you could be a female in the dream, and vice versa. You may be older or younger, of a different ethnicity, from another time period, or even an alien. This person in your dream doesn't look like you; nonetheless, there's an inner knowing that it is you.

This differs from Carl Jung's concept of how everyone in your dream *is an aspect of yourself*, which I went over in Chapter Two. Rather, in this dream category, you look different, while the other characters in your dream are family, friends, and other people you're connected with. These characters might be from today or another timeline, and *are separate from you*.

In this chapter, I'll go over types of dreams when you look different.

Same Person, Different Looks

These three dreams are to help you understand how you can look different, but it's you. Two dreams are from clients and one dream is from me.

Dream One – Different Age

A young female client in her twenties had the following dream:

I was viewing a woman in her 70s or 80s with long gray, straight hair. She was walking up a steep mountain and was two-thirds up. Then I was the old woman inside the body I had just seen. I felt happy, not tired, and enjoyed just being. I had an inner knowing of how one day I will make it to the top.

Interpretation

My client was seeing her future self, who had accomplished much. However, there's always something new to overcome and goals to achieve. It's important to enjoy each moment. She has much time, so she didn't need to rush. One day, she'll make it to the top. Perhaps the top is when she passes and goes to Heaven.

Dream Two – Alternate Reality

Here's a dream from when I was single in my early thirties:

It was me with short hair in a clothing style I wouldn't wear. I was about to get a cup of coffee from the store when I saw my husband's truck from the landscaping company he owned.

In the next scene, he's sitting in his truck and I'm talking to him through the driver's side window. My heart was full of love as I listened to him and thought about how handsome he was.

Interpretation

Upon awakening, there was a part of me who wished this handsome man would come into my life. I felt sad at the time because I knew it wasn't really me as I wouldn't wear those clothes and never cut my hair that short. Another sign it was not me, but *an alternate reality of Pamela,* was how domesticated this version behaved towards her husband. I can't prove if it was an imagined reality or an actual different plane on another Earth. It didn't matter because the important message I got from the dream was to be who I am, whether I'm single or in a relationship. FYI I never met this man in my current existence.

Dream Three - Alien Planet

An older man in his seventies had the following dream:

I was somewhere I'd never been. The buildings were made out of some material I had never seen before. I went to reach out to touch it to find out what it was. To my shock, I had a child's hand and

97

arm. In an instant, I was looking down on this girl. She was a child with a translucent body.

It was crystal clear to me this little girl was me in the future on another planet. I'm not sure how I knew that, but I knew it was for real.

Interpretation

A more logical interpretation was this man was getting in touch with his inner child's feminine side, which felt alien to him. Yet I felt his energy and his inner knowing. My gut knew this was him in a future life on another planet, or at least not our current Earth.

Are These Dreams Factual?

As I mentioned earlier, these types of dreams can't be proven. A logical or scientifically minded person could say the young woman wanted more wisdom, I wanted to be married, and the old man wanted to feel young again. Yes, this is one way of looking at it.

Another way of viewing these dreams is to consider how it helps each person.

1. The younger woman has hope for the future. It inspired her to continue her studies, although she will change her major to an area that will make her happy. Her parents will complain; however, she realizes standing up for herself is part of her journey

     up the mountain.

2. My dream reminded me to be myself whenever I got into a committed relationship. It also inspired me to keep my hair long as I look awful in short hair.

3. For the older man, it reinforced his belief in life after death, reincarnation, and how each day is a gift.

Besides different ages, alternate realities, and alien planets, there are also past life dreams.

Past Lives

Before going into past life dreams, I like to point out that past lives are an ongoing study by psychologists and medical doctors. There are lots of interesting cases of children remembering their past lives. Children have shared facts about their other lives, even though they had no way of knowing this information.

Hypnosis is one method used in studying past lives. Amazing information has come from past life regression. If this topic fascinates you, then I encourage you to research it. I recommend starting with Brian Weiss as I have read his books, heard him speak at a conference, and met him in an elevator. Back in 1980, Weiss didn't believe in past lives until one of his hypnosis patients gave details about her past life, then about his personal life. Thus, changing his life forever.

Personally, past lives always felt right to me. My Higher Source allows me to make mistakes to learn lessons and some lessons need to be repeated over and over and over... for me to finally comprehend it. I just couldn't believe that a loving Higher Source would just give me one shot and if I messed up (a religious philosophy) – my soul was damned for eternity. Plus, I've had past lives recalled in dreams, meditation, and hypnotic regressions. Therefore, after becoming an advanced hypnotherapist in the early nineties, I also became certified in past life regression.

Some people wonder why we can't remember all our past lives. One reason is that we would have a hard time staying in the present and focusing on this lifetime. Another reason is that it could cause mental illness and other hardships. This is why a past life can only be known when a person needs it. It's easier to recall past lives through hypnotic regression and during dreams.

Past Life Dreams

Past life dreams stand out and are easy to recall. Often, they come to explain why you are experiencing an obstacle in your life and the need to resolve it.

For example, a woman has an intense fear of water. She refuses to go anywhere near water and won't even take a bath. She can barely tolerate showers. Her company is promoting her to a position she always wanted, although it's in Hawaii. The woman wants her dream job, yet is terrified. That night she prays for help and dreamed the following dream:

She's a rich, noblewoman who lives in a castle on the English coastline. Pirates invade the castle while she is in a cast iron bath.

The captain bursts into her room, removes her wedding ring, and then pushes her head into the water until she drowns.

She awakens with feelings of relief and freedom. She wonders if it was truly her in the dream. Then decides to test her fear of water by filling the bathtub. For the first time in her life, she enjoys a bath. Afterwards, she leaves her boss a voicemail accepting the job.

Eight Signs of a Past Life Dream

1. You know it's you, but you are another person.
2. The scenery is from a time in the past.
3. People are wearing old-fashioned clothing.
4. You are another ethnicity or sex.
5. Belief systems differ from today's beliefs.
6. Somehow you know the year and it's in the past.
7. Words are being spoken in another language or an older English format, yet you understand the words.
8. There aren't any modern conveniences. For example, communication is done by a messenger on horseback, by handwriting a letter, or by a rotary phone.

Past Life Dreams Help You With

These are eight examples of how past life dreams can assist you to better understanding your present life.

1. Health problems.
2. Irrational fears.

3. Issues in your life.
4. Unique characteristic or traits.
5. Instant attraction or dislike to someone.
6. Natural, effortless talents.
7. Attraction or revulsion to a culture or time period.
8. Lifetime work to accomplish.

So, Is It You?

Is the character in your dream actually you? I can't answer this for you. You must answer this question for yourself. Your inner wisdom will reveal in its *own unique manner* if it is you in a past life, a different plane, another planet, or a future life.

The next and last chapter provides insights on how to use and integrate your dreams' wisdom into your life.

Chapter Nine

Nighttime Messages, Daytime Wisdom

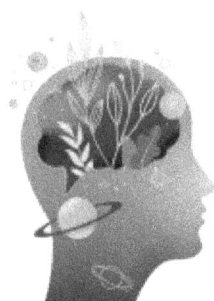

A former coach of mine helped me come up with my slogan *Nighttime Messages, Daytime Wisdom*. She first thought of nighttime visions, yet visions didn't feel right to me. Dreams are more than visions. They are also our emotions, our five senses, and our different psychic abilities.

If we do nothing with our nighttime messages, then it's worthless to recall and record our dreams. It's similar to an alcoholic who realizes they have a drinking problem and knows their life would be better if they stop drinking. Nonetheless, if the alcoholic doesn't take action with the knowledge of being addicted to alcohol and continues to drink, they will continue to be stuck in a rut.

The insights from our dreams are wisdom to be used during the daytime. Dreams are self-therapy for creating changes to enrich our lives. We need to take this knowledge seriously and put it into action for our personal and spiritual growth. This isn't always easy, although it's better than suffering in the same old, same old.

How to Use the Dream's Wisdom

I went over how to use your nighttime messages to help your relationships in Chapter Five. And in Chapter Six, we looked at the gift of knowing of an upcoming death because you can prepare and take action. Let's use three new dreams to showcase this even more.

Dream One of a Deceased Father

One of my clients (I will call her Linda) had a dream where she felt upset because her deceased father was running away from her. Do you remember in Chapter Seven I went over the three types of deceased dreams? Linda's dream was an issue dream because her father wasn't visiting her and she had negative emotions. The following are three meanings for her dream:

1. She hasn't dealt with her father's death.
2. The dream is to help Linda through the process of living without her father.
3. Her abandonment issues with her father were caused by his death or an issue in the past.

This dream's wisdom was for Linda to go further into grief over the death of her father and any childhood issues from the past. Working on her grief and abandonment issues will enable Linda to live without her father. Please note, this is not an overnight process, and she, or anyone else experiencing this, needs to take as much time as needed.

Dream Two of Dresser Drawers

Another client's (whom I'll call Sally) mother had recently passed. Sally dreamed she was going through her mother's dresser drawers and finding all kinds of treasure. Here are three meanings for her dream:

1. Sally needs to go through her mother's belongings to find items that she will treasure.
2. She is looking for positive traits of her mother, which Sally can also find in herself.
3. Her mother has secrets that she will find out about.

Sally can use the wisdom of these nighttime messages when she has to go through her mother's belongings, where she may discover treasured items or secrets she didn't know about her mother. It's also important for Sally to ponder and journal all the positive traits about her mother that she can discover within herself. This will help Sally through the grief process.

Dream Three for a Solution

Here's a personal dream of mine I had a decade ago. I was working the psychic lines and was unhappy there. Sadly, a large percentage of clients on these lines were like the alcoholic I mentioned earlier. They had plenty of questions, but didn't want to do the work once they knew the answers. I asked my angels for a solution dream. The dream was about a bookkeeping job I had in the late 80s.

When I woke up, I understood the nighttime message because I was very unhappy at my former job. What a relief it was when I quit that bookkeeping job. If I had enjoyed working there, the dream would have had a different meaning. Now I needed to take the dream's wisdom and put it into action. This is what I did:

1. Asked my life mate if it was okay for me to leave the lines.
2. Gave notice to these psychic lines.
3. Focused on expanding my business.

Self-employment is a work in progress... My dreams guide me on the next steps to take in business. Whether that's writing a book, doing a Kickstarter, joining an organization, or subcontracting for better psychic lines.

Process of Using Your Dreams' Wisdom

A dream journal is a useful tool for dream interpretation. You can use paper and pen, a dream journal app, an audio or video recorder, or other methods to record your dreams. It's useful to flip back to see recurring themes, symbols, and messages.

Your dream journal is also the place for recording possible interpretations of dreams.

In Your Dream Journal

When you review your journal, check to see how your dream meanings relate to:

- Upbringing and experiences.
- Present problems or situations.
- Hopes and goals for the future.

These are clues to the meaning and solutions. Take the earlier example of my solution dream. My dislike and experiences of my past job in the dream were a sign that my present work on the psychic lines wasn't working and I needed to leave. Then it was time to use the dream's message and take the steps for the future.

Not all dreams will be connected to your past, present, and future. Dreams about the past will have to connect to the present or future in some manner. Sometimes your dream is just about the present, yet there might be work you need to do for the future. Precognitive dreams are obviously for your future, but you may need to prepare or stop doing something in the present.

Whatever the daytime wisdom is, please record it in your dream journal.

Daytime Action

Sadly, action is where many people procrastinate. Your situation might not be as dire as the alcoholic metaphor I gave earlier in the chapter. However, when you don't take action, like a log blocking the flow of water, your life will become stagnate and could eventually stink or become toxic similar to stalled water.

My former hypnosis teacher's philosophy was you can't stop smoking, lose weight, and learn how to bake a cake at the same time. To make a change, it is important to focus on one or two things at a time. We can break actions down into baby steps.

If your dream's meaning was for you to start dating again, and you don't feel ready, don't put up an online dating profile right away. Instead, take any of these seven steps:

1. Review your past relationship to see if there are unresolved issues.
2. Resolve your issues.
3. Do a makeover if it feels right, then lose weight, get a new hairstyle, or buy new clothes.
4. Participate in group activities or clubs.
5. Go out with friends.
6. Ask friends to set you up with someone.
7. Join an online dating site.

Use your dream journal to break down your action steps. For example, when you need to:

- Confront someone.
- Work on a relationship.

- Find a new job.
- Move to another area.
- Create a new business.
- Learn a new skill.
- Give up a habit or addiction.

Whatever your dream's guidance, it's important to begin. There's no guarantee where you will end up; nevertheless, it beats not knowing what could have been.

Your Personal and Spiritual Growth

In Chapter One, I mentioned how dream interpretation will help accelerate our personal and spiritual growth. Wouldn't it be nice if we could have a dream and then our life would change instantly for the better? Our nighttime dreams' messages are important because they give us reality checks, directions, and answers.

You then need to go through the process: going within, breaking out of denial, being honest with yourself, feeling the emotions, taking baby steps, and achieving your goal. Your personal and spiritual growth is hard work, yet it is better than a life of misery from remaining the same.

Your life will improve with nighttime messages when you implement them into daytime wisdom. Remember, personal and spiritual growth is an ongoing process as long as you are alive. Or perhaps it continues beyond your lifetime?

Conclusion

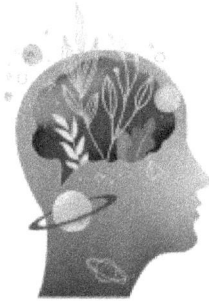

Thank you for reading my book, and what an honor it has been to be a part of your dream interpretation journey! I encourage you to continue going within to understand your personal dream language and dream meanings.

You can find a wealth of dream interpretation knowledge on the internet through articles, books, podcasts, and videos. Remember, these are based on people's research, knowledge, experiences, and opinions. Therefore, it's important to listen to your intuition about what information resonates with you. Then test this technique to find out if it works for you. If it does, great, and if it doesn't, look for another system. Your dream path will be unique to others, so use the method that suits you best.

If you would like to continue working with me, I love to help you with my services or products. Please visit my website at https://pamelacummins.com/

I wish you many sweet dreams that will accelerate your personal and spiritual growth.

Blessings,

Pamela Cummins

About the Author

Pamela Cummins is an expert dream interpreter, spiritual growth coach, psychic, author, and oracle creator. She helps her clients accelerate their personal and spiritual growth through understanding their dream meanings and accessing their inner wisdom.

Learn more about her at https://pamelacummins.com/

More Books by Pamela Cummins

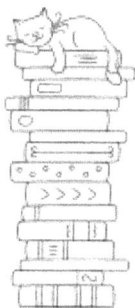

The following books are available at many book realtors. For the link to your favorite bookstore, please visit https://pamelacummins.com/books/

Learn the Secret Language of Dreams

Do you know that your dreams are special and unique? But if you don't understand their meaning, you are missing out on vital information. Because every night your subconscious mind sends you messages to help you solve problems, improve relationships, and teach you how to create a higher quality of life. The key is to learn how to decipher them and that is how Pamela Cummins, dream and relationship expert, can help you. *Learn the Secret Language of Dreams* is designed to give you the ability to understand the meanings of your own dreams.

Symbolism in dreams is not a "one size fits all." One symbol can mean many things. In order to understand the nature of dream symbolism more clearly, you will need to know what category your dream fits into. This eBook will help you identify the different dream styles so you can recognize what part of your life the dream message is for. Once you know the category of your dream, it will be easier to interpret your unique personal symbolism.

Got Dreams? Discover Your Ideal Dream Journal

Have you ever told yourself upon awakening that you will remember the dream you just had, but forgot large chunks of it within minutes? This is why it's imperative to record your dreams. Yet, what journal style would work best for you?

Expert dream interpreter, Pamela Cummins, has your answer and more. *In Got Dreams? Discover Your Ideal Dream Journal,* you will learn: nine different types of dream journals, the benefits of journaling your dreams, how dream interpretation will empower your life, and a glimpse into understanding your dream meanings.

Personal Growth Affirmations

Do you desire more happiness and peace in your daily living? Did you know that you can have the life you always dreamed of? Change is possible; however, all transition starts within. *Personal Growth Affirmations* will motivate you to begin the process of your transformation journey with fifty-two weekly affirmations to be used for self-help and/or meditation.

Some of the topics are: self-love, forgiveness, patience, gratitude, boundaries, meditation, connecting with a Higher Source, the ups and downs of living, and much more. The affirmations have questions to inspire reflection, action steps to help you transcend, and a short mantra to be chanted any time you feel the need. Manifestation of your aspirations becomes reality by applying the wisdom of each affirmation. Now is the time to start your journey...

This Curly Woman Went Gray

A dream about her dead hairstylist inspired Pamela to stop dyeing her hair. She discovered growing out her silvers is NOT an easy path, yet filled with many powerful lessons. Pamela shares what she learned to ease your journey, whether you're thinking about starting or already transitioning to gray hair.

In *This Curly Woman Went Gray*, you will learn three methods to choose from to return to your natural hair color. There are tips to help you go through the awkward beginning stages. They include how to recognize the four types of unsolicited advice and what actions to take with these polite hair trolls. During this voyage, you may need to look at your hair story and use the steps provided to heal any hair trauma.

There's also a chapter about how to take care of your curly hair. Whatever texture your hair is, this eBook is for you.

Pamela's Love Collection

What does self-love, the Three F's, and "He has to be spiritual" have in common? They are all in *Pamela's Love Collection*. Love is always in the air, but often it's just out of our grasp. Whether you're single or in a relationship, it's time to reach for it. You will learn how to recognize the signs of healthy love and what to do with it.

Spiritual growth intuitive, Pamela Cummins, selected twelve of her articles, blogs, and columns that show different aspects of self-love and love relationships. You'll discover lots of great tips and steps to implement right away. If you desire a happy, healthy, and loving relationship, this eBook is a must read.

Insights for Singles: Steps to Find Everlasting Love

Insights for Singles: Steps to Find Everlasting Love delivers insights to help readers reach their highest potential, learn to think positively, recognize red flags, how to let go of a relationship, improve communication skills, and understand how to attract and proceed with the "Right One." Whether you need to learn to "Keep your pants on" or "My fantasy is not reality," singles will find plenty of potent insight and proven solutions in this eBook.

After each insights there are questions singles can use as a guide to reflect on, use in meditation, and/or write answers in a journal. These questions can also be used for deep soul searching.

Psychic Wisdom on Love and Relationships

Read how a psychic's insights into the spirit world give knowledge to transform your love life. Pamela noticed patterns with the questions her clients asked. Will I ever find love? When is he going to call? How can I get my mate to open up? You may have similar questions. Maybe you're sick of horrible dates and relationships, or you are bored and unsatisfied in your relationship?

Then Psychic Wisdom on Love and Relationships is for you. Pamela Cummins' guides often repeat the message to focus on yourself for a better and healthier relationship. You will learn other valuable information from the spirit world, too. If you are ready for a love of a lifetime, it's time to take a journey of self-love, boundaries, intuition, communication skills, and more.